SINK YOUR TEETH INTO
DINOSAURS!

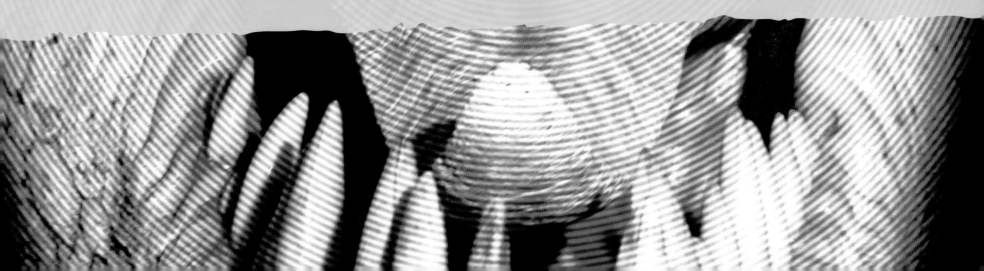

CONTENTS

FOSSIL FINDS

Dinosaurs first roamed Earth at the beginning of the Mesozoic era, more than **245 MILLION YEARS AGO.** For the next 180 million years, they lived and thrived in an amazing prehistoric environment—until a catastrophic mass extinction wiped them out.

How can we tell what dinosaurs looked like? And how do we know about the ways they interacted with each other?

FOSSILS—remains preserved from a past geologic age—give scientists the answers to many of these questions, and dinosaur teeth hold especially important clues to how these animals lived.

Come and peer inside the jaws of dinosaurs, from little Coelophysis to towering Apatosaurus and terrifying T. rex, and see what you can discover about the lives of these fascinating and fearsome creatures.

THE FOSSIL EVIDENCE

More than 1,000 species of dinosaurs have been discovered so far through fossil finds worldwide. Thanks to these remains, scientists are able to determine an amazing amount of information.

SOLVING CLUES

Using just a few pieces of bone, scientists can tell how big an animal was and what it might have looked like. For example, footprints and leg bones hold answers to how fast a dinosaur could run, and scientists can also figure out the size of a dinosaur's brain by examining its skull. Computer models based on these fossils can also be created to explore the answers to questions such as how fast could Diplodocus whip its tail, or how did Allosaurus eat its meals.

DENTAL RECORDS

Teeth are very valuable clues to discovering how dinosaurs lived. In fact, some dinosaurs, like meat-eater Deinodon, are known only because of their teeth! Why are there so many fossils of teeth? Firstly, teeth fossilize more easily than other materials. Secondly, the jaws of some types of dinosaurs held rows of replacement teeth. Whenever a tooth fell out another one moved in to take its place, and these dinosaurs lost many teeth throughout their lifetime.

WHAT'S FOR LUNCH?

Based on the shape and size of a fossilized tooth, we can put together a picture of the dinosaur's diet.

MEAT EATERS often had sharp, knifelike teeth that helped them wound prey by slashing or curved teeth that could help them grip slippery or wriggly prey.

PLANT EATERS usually had beaks or thin, rakelike teeth for clipping and stripping leaves or thin, ridged teeth for grinding plants.

BIG TEETH FOR A BIG APPETITE

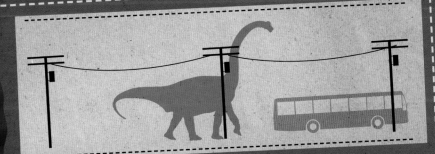

← about 45 feet (13.7 m) →

Many dinosaurs were big—**REALLY BIG!** Some of the dinosaurs you'll read about in this book were as long as city buses or as tall as telephone poles. To get that big, they probably had to eat constantly.

SAUROPODS: Scientists think these large plant-eating dinosaurs could have consumed more than 100,000 calories a day. We'd have to eat 3,333 cups of broccoli to consume that many calories!

THEROPODS: Big meat eaters like Tyrannosaurus rex could chomp more than 500 pounds (227 kg) of meat in one bite.

DINOSAUR
TYRANNOSAURUS REX

PRONUNCIATION: TIE-RAN-OH-SORE-USS RECKS

FOSSIL FILE 1

T. rex had a mouthful of nearly 60 teeth, some of which were banana shaped and over six inches (15.2 cm) long. Some scientists think this meat eater actively preyed on small- and medium-sized dinosaurs, as well as weaker large dinosaurs.

DINO STATS!

NAME MEANS: TYRANT LIZARD KING

SIZE: 43 FEET *(13 M)* IN LENGTH, 20 FEET *(6 M)* TALL

YIKES!!!

AVG WOMAN:
5 FT. 4 IN. *(1.62 M)*

WEIGHT: 14,000 POUNDS *(6,350 KG)*

PERIOD: LATE CRETACEOUS, 85–65 MILLION YEARS AGO

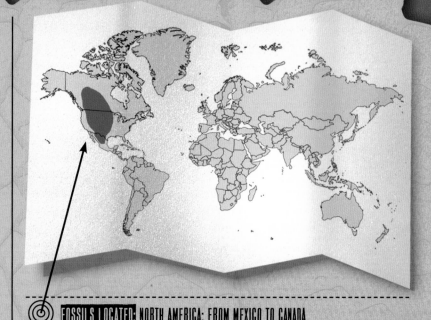

FOSSILS LOCATED: NORTH AMERICA: FROM MEXICO TO CANADA

LIZARD KING

Hundreds of T. rex fossils have been discovered, including a fossilized Hadrosaur with a T. rex tooth stuck in its healed bone. This means that the Hadrosaur survived the attack—and that the T. rex lost a tooth! Some scientists think T. rex was a scavenger, rather than a predator, because of its small arms and little eyes. Either way, T. rex definitely ate Triceratops: fossilized T. rex droppings have contained bits of Triceratops bone.

DINOSAUR
APATOSAURUS

PRONUNCIATION: AH-PAH-TOW-SORE-US

Apatosaurus teeth are often described as being like pencils. Thin and blunt, these teeth probably didn't help Apatosaurus chew. Scientists think that this dinosaur, like Barosaurus and many of its fellow large sauropods, may have swallowed stones to help it grind up and digest food.

DINOSTATS!

NAME MEANS: FALSE LIZARD

SIZE: 75 FEET *(23 M)* IN LENGTH, 30 FEET *(9 M)* TALL

AVG HUMAN: 5 FT. 8 IN. *(1.72 M)*

WEIGHT: 40,000–75,000 POUNDS *(18,144–34,019 KG)*

PERIOD: LATE JURASSIC, 154–150 MILLION YEARS AGO

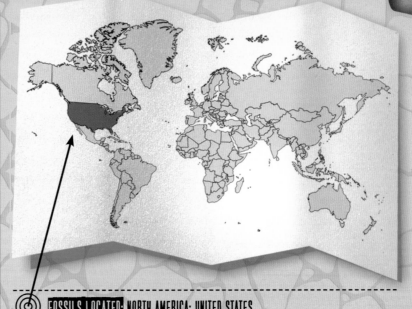

◎ **FOSSILS LOCATED:** NORTH AMERICA: UNITED STATES

LOUISE, THE DINO

Apatosaurus's scientific name, *Apatosaurus louisae*, comes from Louise Carnegie, wife of Andrew Carnegie, a wealthy industrialist who funded many excavations in the early 1900s. The most complete Apatosaurus skeleton includes an intact skull and is on display at the Carnegie Museum of Natural History in Pittsburgh, Pennsylvania. This plant eater was huge: a recently uncovered thighbone stands 6 feet (1.8 m) tall, just a few inches larger than an average male human.

DINOSAUR
EUOPLOCEPHALUS

PRONUNCIATION: YOO-OH-PLO-SEF-AH-LUSS

FOSSIL FILE 3

An herbivore, Euoplocephalus had about 40 small teeth. As the dinosaur chewed, the teeth would grind up the cycads, ferns, and other low-growing plants that made up its diet.

DINOSTATS!

NAME MEANS: WELL-ARMORED HEAD

SIZE: 20 FEET (6 M) IN LENGTH, 6.5 FEET (2 M) TALL

UH OH...

AVG HUMAN:
5 FT. 8 IN. (1.72 M)

WEIGHT: 4,000 POUNDS (1,814 KG)

PERIOD: LATE CRETACEOUS, 99–65 MILLION YEARS AGO

FOSSILS LOCATED: NORTH AMERICA: CANADA AND UNITED STATES

ARMORED WARRIOR

Like its fellow Ankylosauria (armored dinosaurs), Euoplocephalus resembled a big turtle covered with protective spikes and bony plates—even on its eyelids. Although scientists deduce what most dinosaurs looked like based on bits and pieces of fossilized skeletons, dozens of Euoplocephalus fossils have been found, including some nearly complete skeletons with their armor still in place. This means we know almost exactly what they looked like.

DINOSAUR

VELOCIRAPTOR

PRONUNCIATION: veh-LOSS-ih-RAP-tor

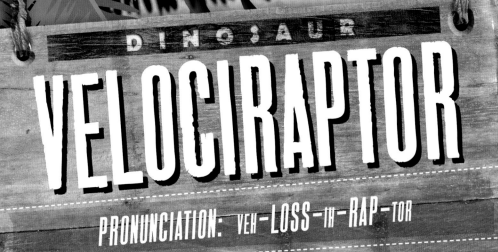

FOSSIL FILE 4

Velociraptor's jaws were lined with about 15 curved, knifelike teeth on each side. Razor-sharp, they were perfect for hooking into prey and chomping. Fossil evidence suggests that Velociraptor was likely both a scavenger and a predator.

DINOSTATS!

NAME MEANS: FAST ROBBER

SIZE: 6 FEET *(1.8 M)* IN LENGTH, 2.5 FEET *(0.8 M)* TALL

ARGH!!!

AVG HUMAN:
5 FT. 8 IN. (1.72 M)

WEIGHT: 50–100 POUNDS *(23–45 KG)*

PERIOD: LATE CRETACEOUS, 99–65 MILLION YEARS AGO

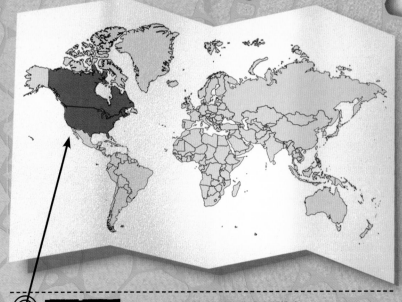

FOSSILS LOCATED: NORTH AMERICA: CANADA AND UNITED STATES

HUNGRY HUNTER

Velociraptor wasn't large, but it was deadly. With sharp teeth and a long, 3.5-inch (9 cm) claw on the middle toe of each foot, it was able to slash and grasp prey. A large brain in relation to its body size suggests it was intelligent, with good hearing, sight, and smell—keen senses for hunting. Fast and nimble, Velociraptor could run at speeds of up to 25 mph (40 kph), easily outpacing its victims.

DINOSAUR
MAJUNGASAURUS

PRONUNCIATION: MAH-JUNG-AH-SORE-USS

FOSSIL FILE 5

Majungasaurus had a shorter, rounder jaw than other big dinosaur predators. Because of this, and because of the shape of its teeth, Majungasaurus likely killed its prey by clamping down in a bite and holding, rather than just slashing and tearing at flesh.

DINOSTATS!

NAME MEANS: MADAGASCAN LIZARD

SIZE: 20 FEET (6 M) IN LENGTH, 11.5 FEET (3.5 M) TALL

YIKES!!!

AVG HUMAN:
5 FT. 8 IN. (1.72 M)

WEIGHT: 2,400 POUNDS (1,089 KG)

PERIOD: LATE CRETACEOUS, 70–65 MILLION YEARS AGO

FOSSILS LOCATED: AFRICA: MADAGASCAR

CANNIBAL LIZARD?

Majungasaurus sported a small single horn on its head. Though it walked on two powerful legs, Majungasaurus had two stubby arms, with four nubby, clawless fingers. Some scientists think its arms were completely useless and may have just hung there. Fossilized Majungasaurus bones have been found with teeth marks that match the bite of other Majungasauruses—suggesting these dinosaurs might have preyed on their own species!

DINOSAUR

THERIZINOSAURUS

PRONUNCIATION: THAIR–AH–ZEEN–OH–SORE–US

FOSSIL FILE ... 6

The team that found the first Therizinosaurus claws thought they had discovered an ancient turtle. Only incomplete skeletons and skulls have been found, so scientists can only guess what Therizinosaurus ate. However, by examining these fossils and those of related dinosaurs, scientists now think Therizinosaurus was an herbivorous theropod.

DINOSTATS!

NAME MEANS: SCYTHE LIZARD

SIZE: 36 FEET (11 M) IN LENGTH, 20—23 FEET (6—7 M) TALL

RUN!!!

AVG HUMAN:
5 FT. 8 IN. (1.72 M)

WEIGHT: 10,500 POUNDS (4,700 KG)

PERIOD: CRETACEOUS, 85—70 MILLION YEARS AGO

⊚ FOSSILS LOCATED: MONGOLIA

THE CLAWS

Strange. Weird. Those are the words that come up again and again when scientists describe Therizinosaurus. This dinosaur appears to be an extreme jumble of different dinosaur features. It had long, feather-covered arms ending in superlong claws, more feathers growing in a fan on its tail, spikes, and a big belly. Add to all this its odd feet that sported four toes to support its weight, instead of a theropod's usual three. What kind of dinosaur was Therizinosaurus? Scientists say Therizinosaurus was one of the last and largest of a group of giant plant eaters that are thought to be descended from meat eaters.

DINOSAUR
HERRERASAURUS

PRONUNCIATION: HER–RARE–UH–SORE–USS

FOSSIL FILE 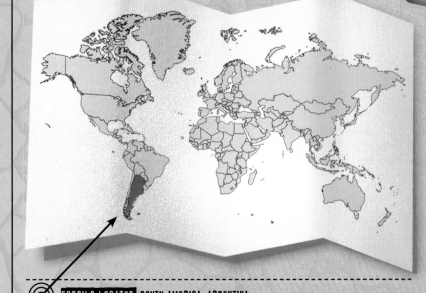 7

Herrerasaurus's long teeth turn toward the back of its jaws and would have allowed it to grasp and hold on to struggling prey, likely small herbivores. It also had a hinged jaw that gave it a big bite.

DINOSTATS!

NAME MEANS: HERRERA'S LIZARD

SIZE: 15 FEET *(4.6 M)* IN LENGTH, 3.5 FEET *(1 M)* TALL

AVG HUMAN: 5 FT. 8 IN. *(1.72 M)*

WEIGHT: 450 POUNDS *(204 KG)*

PERIOD: TRIASSIC, 230–220 MILLION YEARS AGO

FOSSILS LOCATED: SOUTH AMERICA: ARGENTINA

THE FIRST PREDATOR

One of the very first dinosaurs, and the earliest known meat-eating dinosaur, Herrerasaurus was a top predator of the Triassic age, when dinosaurs were still rare. Herrerasaurus ran on powerful back legs and had strong hands with three long-clawed fingers, which scientists think it used to grasp and rip at prey. This carnivore was named after farmer Victorino Herrera, who uncovered the first Herrerasaurus bones in the 1960s.

DINOSAUR
SPINOSAURUS

PRONUNCIATION: SPY-no-SORE-uss

FOSSIL FILE 8

Spinosaurus's head was 6 feet (1.8 m) long, with huge jaws. It had a mouthful of sharp, straight teeth, perfect for snaring big, slippery fish—imagine a modern-day crocodile's jaws, only much, much bigger.

DINOSTATS!

NAME MEANS: SPINE LIZARD

SIZE: 56 FEET (17 M) IN LENGTH, 22 FEET (7 M) TALL

YIKES!!!

AVG HUMAN:
5 FT. 8 IN. (1.72 M)

WEIGHT: 14,000 POUNDS (6,350 KG)

PERIOD: MIDDLE CRETACEOUS, 112–97 MILLION YEARS AGO

FOSSILS LOCATED: AFRICA

DINO SWIMMER

Spinosaurus is named for the tall spikes down its back. They supported a huge sail, which may have helped the animal regulate its body temperature. It was the largest meat eater ever on land, even bigger than T. rex, but recent fossil evidence shows that Spinosaurus was a water dinosaur, too—the first swimming dinosaur ever discovered. Fossils of this monstrous predator have been found in the Sahara desert, which was marshy swampland and watershed during the Middle Cretaceous period.

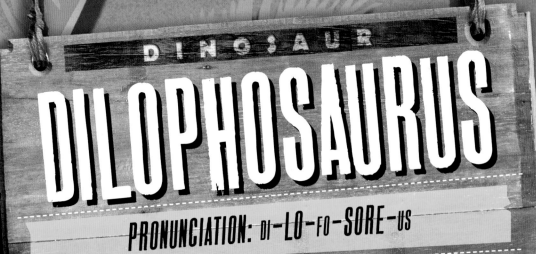

DINOSAUR
DILOPHOSAURUS

PRONUNCIATION: DI-LO-FO-SORE-US

FOSSIL FILE 9

Dilophosaurus had about 30 sharp, pointy teeth—a few of which also had knifelike edges. The teeth got smaller toward the front of the jaw, where Dilophosaurus skulls have a gap. Dilophosaurus's teeth were thin at the bottom, which suggests they broke off easily.

DINOSTATS!

NAME MEANS: DOUBLE-CRESTED LIZARD

SIZE: 23 FEET (7 M) IN LENGTH, 8 FEET (2.5 M) TALL

HELP!!!

AVG WOMAN:
5 FT. 4 IN. (1.62 M)

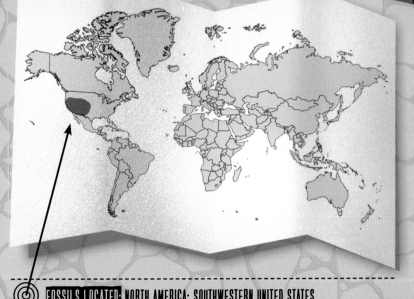

WEIGHT: 1,100 POUNDS (499 KG)

FOSSILS LOCATED: NORTH AMERICA: SOUTHWESTERN UNITED STATES

PERIOD: EARLY JURASSIC, 200–190 MILLION YEARS AGO

PACK HUNTERS?

Dilophosaurus is named for the two thin, bony crests at the top of its skull. It had long, sharp claws, a movable thumb, and strong legs. Some scientists think this dinosaur used its hands and feet to slash and claw prey rather than biting it with its weak jaws. Dilophosaurus skeletons have been discovered near each other, leading scientists to believe that these dinosaurs may have hunted in packs.

DINOSAUR
TROODON

PRONUNCIATION: TROH-UH-DON

FOSSIL FILE 10

Troodon got its name from the first fossil specimen ever discovered of this dinosaur— one tooth with unusual grooves, found in 1855. The name means "wounding tooth." Among other Troodon fossils discovered since that time is a lower jaw that showed the dinosaur had 35 teeth on each side, more than any other theropod.

DINOSTATS!

NAME MEANS: WOUNDING TOOTH

SIZE: 6.5 FEET (2 M) IN LENGTH, 3 FEET (.91 M) TALL

AVG WOMAN:
5 FT. 4 IN. (1.62 M)

WEIGHT: 100 POUNDS (50 KG)

PERIOD: CRETACEOUS, 78—76 MILLION YEARS AGO

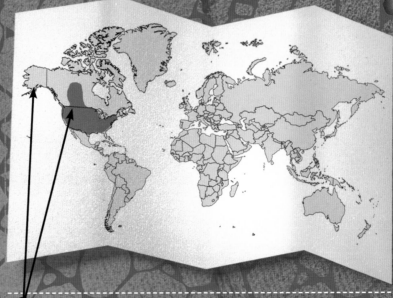

FOSSILS LOCATED: NORTH AMERICA: MONTANA, WYOMING, ALASKA, ALBERTA, CANADA

SMART HUNTER

Troodon was small in size, but it had something big going for it: a brain the size of a golf ball. That may not sound large, but compared to its body, it suggests that Troodon may have been one of the smartest dinosaurs ever—perhaps with the intelligence of a modern bird.

Was this clever dinosaur a sauropod or theropod? It had the long, sharp claws of a meat eater, but it had several different shapes of teeth, including serrated or jagged teeth, which are good for shredding leaves. This may mean it was an omnivore, feeding on both plants and animals, such as lizards and mammals, as well as insects.

DINOSAUR DIPLODOCUS

PRONUNCIATION: DI-PLOD-OH-KUSS

FOSSIL FILE 11

Diplodocus had about 40 thin teeth, grouped toward the front of its jaws, which were good for stripping leaves. Diplodocus's teeth were replaced about once a month: old teeth fell out and new ones moved into place. This prevented the teeth from wearing down due to Diplodocus's constant eating.

DINO STATS!

NAME MEANS: DOUBLE BEAM

SIZE: 82 FEET *(25 M)* IN LENGTH, 46 FEET *(14 M)* TALL

WHOA!!!

AVG HUMAN:
5 FT. 8 IN. *(1.72 M)*

WEIGHT: 33,000 POUNDS *(15,000 KG)*

PERIOD: JURASSIC, 155–145 MILLION YEARS AGO

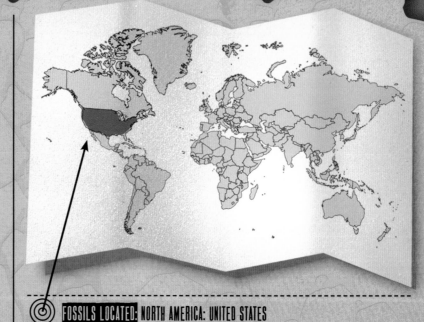

FOSSILS LOCATED: NORTH AMERICA: UNITED STATES

A WHALE OF A TAIL!

Diplodocus's tail was a mighty 45 feet (13.7 m) long, about the length of a humpback whale. Scientists think Diplodocus may have swung its tail like a whip, with the tip reaching speeds of more than 750 mph (1,200 kph). This would have created a sound like a cannon blast to scare away predators. Usually, Diplodocus's tail acted as a counterbalance to its long neck while it grazed for food.

DINOSAUR
STEGOSAURUS

PRONUNCIATION: STEG-OH-SORE-USS

FOSSIL FILE 12

Stegosaurus's bony beak helped it pluck ferns, moss, fruit, palmlike cycads, and other Jurassic plants. It ground up the plant material by chewing with its small, thin teeth. Based on the size of its head and jaws, scientists think that a Stegosaurus had a surprisingly weak bite: a modern dog could probably chomp harder.

DINOSTATS!

NAME MEANS: ROOF LIZARD

SIZE: 30 FEET (9 M) IN LENGTH, 12 FEET (3.7 M) TALL

WANT A TREAT?

AVG MAN:
5 FT. 10 IN. (1.78 M)

WEIGHT: 6,800 POUNDS (3,084 KG)

PERIOD: LATE JURASSIC, 150–144 MILLION YEARS AGO

FOSSILS LOCATED: NORTH AMERICA: SOUTHWESTERN UNITED STATES; EUROPE: PORTUGAL

ARMORED WARRIOR

Stegosaurus stands out thanks to the row of huge plates—some almost 2 feet (0.6 m) tall—along its back. Too thin to protect it against predators, the plates were probably used to attract mates. Scientists think it swung its spiked tail quickly to strike attackers. One Allosaurus fossil has a hole in its tailbone about the same size and shape as a stegosaurus tail spike. Ouch!

DINOSAUR MICRORAPTOR

PRONUNCIATION: MY-crow-RAP-tor

Microraptor probably wasn't able to run or walk across the ground. Why? Its hind-leg feathers were long. Microraptor would have tripped over them with each step it took! So when Microraptor wasn't airborne, it perched in trees.

DINOSTATS!

NAME MEANS: SMALL THIEF

SIZE: 3 FEET (1 M) IN LENGTH

KINDA CUTE?!

AVG MAN:
5 FT. 10 IN. (1.78 M)

WEIGHT: 2 POUNDS (1 KG)

PERIOD: EARLY CRETACEOUS, 125—122 MILLION YEARS AGO

FOSSILS LOCATED: CHINA: LIAONING PROVINCE

A LINK TO BIRDS?

In 2002, scientists discovered one of the smallest dinosaurs known. Microraptor was only 3 feet (1 m) long from beak to tail. But that wasn't the only interesting thing about this dinosaur. Microraptor had long feathers similar to those of modern birds that fly. In fact, many scientists believe that Microraptor may hold clues to how dinosaurs evolved into birds.

DINOSAUR
GIGANOTOSAURUS

PRONUNCIATION: JI-GA-NO-TOW-SORE-US

Not many Giganotosaurus fossils have been found. But among them is a nearly complete skull, which includes 8-inch-long (20.3 cm) sharp teeth, indicating Giganotosaurus was able to slice into prey.

DINOSTATS!

NAME MEANS: GIANT SOUTHERN LIZARD

SIZE: 41 FEET (12.5 M) IN LENGTH, 16.5 FEET (5 M) TALL

YIKES!!!

AVG HUMAN: 5 FT. 8 IN. (1.72 M)

WEIGHT: 20,000 POUNDS (9,072 KG)

PERIOD: CRETACEOUS, 100—95 MILLION YEARS AGO

FOSSILS LOCATED: SOUTH AMERICA: ARGENTINA

LOOK FAMILIAR?

Giganotosaurus has a close look-alike: Tyrannosaurus rex. Bigger than T. rex, and with three clawed fingers rather than two, Giganotosaurus roamed Earth alongside huge plant-eating dinosaurs. Unlike some other large theropods, which scientists think were scavengers, Giganotosaurus may have been able to actively hunt, attack, and kill gigantic sauropods. Fossilized remains of Argentinosaurus—one of the largest land animals ever, weighing nearly 10 times as much as Giganotosaurus—have been found near this predator.

DINOSAUR

BAROSAURUS

PRONUNCIATION: BARE-oh-SORE-us

A Barosaurus skull has yet to be found, so we don't know for sure what its teeth looked like. But Barosaurus shares many features of other large sauropods, so it's likely that its teeth were similar to those of Apatosaurus or Diplodocus: long and peglike and ideal for stripping leaves from plants.

DINOSTATS!

NAME MEANS: HEAVY LIZARD

SIZE: 80 FEET (24 M) IN LENGTH, 40 FEET (12 M) TALL

BUS LENGTH:
37 FT. (11.28 M)

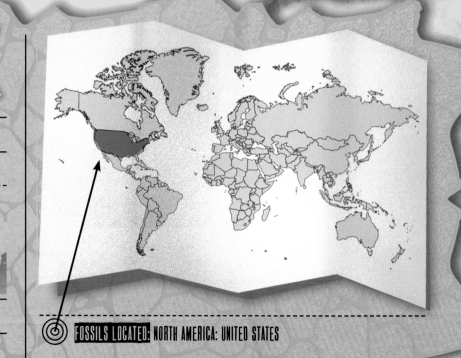

WEIGHT: 44,000 POUNDS (19,958 KG)

PERIOD: LATE JURASSIC, 155–145 MILLION YEARS AGO

FOSSILS LOCATED: NORTH AMERICA: UNITED STATES

STONY STOMACH

Barosaurus was a large plant-eating dinosaur similar to Diplodocus, but with a longer neck and a shorter tail. Not many Barosaurus fossils have been discovered, but those that have include some interesting details. For example, one fossil includes an imprint of what looks like tough and bumpy skin. Another Barosaurus skeleton shows that the animal's stomach contained gastroliths, stones that an animal swallows to help it grind up food.

DINOSAUR
CORYTHOSAURUS

PRONUNCIATION: CORE-ITH-OH-SORE-US

Corythosaurus was a type of duck-billed dinosaur also known as a Hadrosaur. A plant eater, its bill had no teeth. Instead it had cheek teeth—blunt, fan-shaped teeth toward the back of its jaws. Numbering in the hundreds, these cheek teeth ground up food much like human molars do.

DINOSTATS!

NAME MEANS: HELMET LIZARD

SIZE: 30 FEET (9 M) IN LENGTH, 21 FEET (6.4 M) TALL

WANT A TREAT?

AVG HUMAN: 5 FT. 8 IN. (1.72 M)

WEIGHT: 8,860 POUNDS (4,019 KG)

PERIOD: LATE CRETACEOUS, 80–75 MILLION YEARS AGO

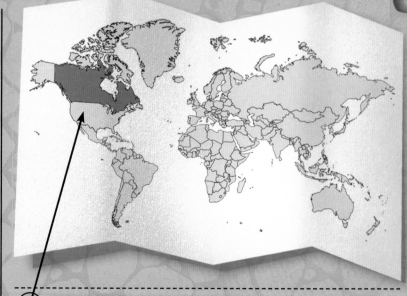

FOSSILS LOCATED: NORTH AMERICA: CANADA

HONKING HELMET

The special rounded crest atop Corythosaurus's head, often called a helmet, held a complex structure of tubes that connected to the animal's nostrils. The exact purpose of these tubes remains unclear, but some scientists think Corythosaurus could blow through them to make loud toots or honks to communicate with other dinosaurs and to warn of predators.

DINOSAUR

MEGALOSAURUS

PRONUNCIATION: MEG-ah-low-SORE-us

The Megalosaurus thighbone found in 1676 was the first dinosaur bone identified anywhere in the world. Later scientists found vertebrae (backbones), leg and hip pieces, and a portion of a lower jaw with a single daggerlike tooth.

DINOSTATS!

NAME MEANS: BIG LIZARD

SIZE: 27–30 FEET *(8–9M)* IN LENGTH, UP TO 10 FEET *(3 M)* TALL

AVG HUMAN:
5 FT. 8 IN. (1.72 M)

WEIGHT: 2,000 POUNDS *(900 KG)*

PERIOD: JURASSIC, 176–161 MILLION YEARS AGO

FOSSILS LOCATED: EUROPE: OXFORDSHIRE, ENGLAND

FIRST FOSSIL

In the middle Jurassic, few creatures messed with Megalosaurus. A top predator with massive weight and power, Megalosaurus was so big that the people who discovered its fossilized thighbone in 1676 thought it belonged to a prehistoric giant.

Megalosaurus was big in terms of scientific importance, too. It was the first dinosaur fossil discovered *and* the first dinosaur to receive a scientific name. Geology professor William Buckland chose the name Megalosaurus in 1824. This big lizard likely ate big prey, such as the gigantic sauropods of the Jurassic.

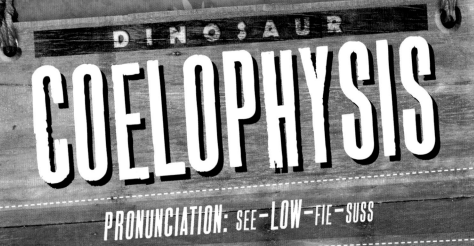

DINOSAUR
COELOPHYSIS

PRONUNCIATION: SEE-LOW-FIE-SUSS

Coelophysis's long, thin jaws were lined with more than 100 small, sharp, and serrated teeth. Coupled with its claws, these teeth helped Coelophysis snatch and grasp prey.

DINOSTATS!

NAME MEANS: HOLLOW FORM

SIZE: 6 FEET (1.8 M) IN LENGTH, 6.5 FEET (2 M) TALL

AVG HUMAN: 5 FT. 8 IN. (1.72 M)

WEIGHT: 45 POUNDS (20 KG)

PERIOD: LATE TRIASSIC, 225–220 MILLION YEARS AGO

FOSSILS LOCATED: NORTH AMERICA: SOUTHWESTERN UNITED STATES

PACK HUNTER

With its thin body, long tail, and narrow head, this slim dinosaur was lightweight and streamlined, able to chase down the quick-moving lizards and small mammals it preyed upon. Coelophysis remains were involved in one of the most famous fossil finds: archaeologists in New Mexico uncovered hundreds of Coelophysis skeletons in one fossil bed. Scientists suspect this dinosaur was a pack hunter, and this particular pack was killed together by a flash flood or other disaster.

ALLOSAURUS

PRONUNCIATION: AL-LOW-SORE-USS

FOSSIL FILE **19**

Allosaurus had a mouthful of about 30 sharp teeth, which it lost and replaced throughout its life. Four inches (10 cm) long and on the sides of its jaws, they curved backward and could hook into flesh when the dinosaur would bite. It's likely that Allosaurus never chewed its food and just gulped down chunks of flesh.

DINOSTATS!

NAME MEANS: DIFFERENT LIZARD

SIZE: 40 FEET (12 M) IN LENGTH, 16 FEET (4.9 M) TALL

YIKES!!!

AVG HUMAN: 5 FT. 8 IN. (1.72 M)

WEIGHT: 3,200 POUNDS (1,451 KG)

PERIOD: JURASSIC, 155-144 MILLION YEARS AGO

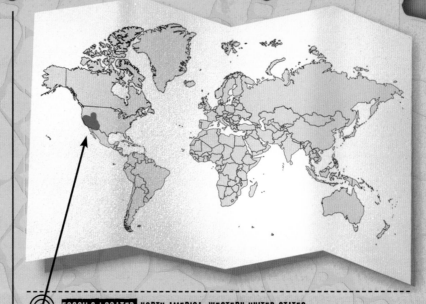

FOSSILS LOCATED: NORTH AMERICA: WESTERN UNITED STATES

JURASSIC ATTACK

With knifelike teeth, sharp claws, and powerful legs, this meat eater was a top predator. Though Allosaurus's arms were on the short side, they were strong compared to most meat eaters' and could be used in attacks on prey such as Stegosaurus and Diplodocus. Computer simulations created from Allosaurus skeletons show that it could move its head and neck quickly and precisely, allowing it to strip flesh off its prey.

DINOSAUR
TRICERATOPS

PRONUNCIATION: TRY-SER-AH-TOPS

FOSSIL FILE 20

Triceratops had a large beak and mouth rimmed with tightly spaced teeth. Its teeth acted like garden shears, clipping through tough plants. Like sharks today, Triceratops's jaws were lined with replacement teeth. Whenever one fell out or wore out, another moved into its place.

DINOSTATS!

NAME MEANS: THREE-HORNED FACE

SIZE: 30 FEET (9 M) IN LENGTH, 10 FEET (3 M) TALL

EEEEP!

AVG HUMAN: 5 FT. 8 IN. (1.72 M)

WEIGHT: 19,800 POUNDS (8,981 KG)

PERIOD: LATE CRETACEOUS, 72–65 MILLION YEARS AGO

FOSSILS LOCATED: NORTH AMERICA: WESTERN UNITED STATES AND CANADA

HELPFUL HORNS

Named after its three horns—which could grow up to 3 feet (0.9 m)—Triceratops was one of the last dinosaurs alive before the mass extinction. Its 8-foot (2.4 m) head held a huge frill, or bony plate, that curved up and grew as the dinosaur did. But the frill and horns weren't just for show; they were also for defense against predators like Tyrannosaurus rex.

WHO LIVED WHEN?

Dinosaurs lived millions of years ago during the Mesozoic era, which is separated into three time periods: the **Triassic**, the **Jurassic**, and the **Cretaceous**. This diagram shows the periods some of the dinosaurs in this book belonged to. It's easy to imagine they all existed at the same time, but Stegosaurus went extinct 60 million years before Tyrannosaurus rex even existed!

TRIASSIC

251–200 million years ago:
Dinosaurs first appeared

HERRERASAURUS

[230–220 million years ago]

COELOPHYSIS

[225–220 million years ago]

JURASSIC

200–145.5 million years ago:
Dinosaurs ruled Earth

DILOPHOSAURUS

[200–190 million years ago]

MEGALOSAURUS

[176–161 million years ago]

APATOSAURUS

[154–150 million years ago]

DIPLODOCUS

[155–145 million years ago]

CRETACEOUS

145.5–65.5 million years ago:
Ended when a mass extinction
wiped out dinosaurs

MICRORAPTOR

[125–122 million years ago]

SPINOSAURUS

[112–97 million years ago]

GIGANOTOSAURUS

[100–95 million years ago]

EUOPLOCEPHALUS

[99–65 million years ago]

BAROSAURUS

[155–145 million years ago]

ALLOSAURUS

[155–144 million years ago]

STEGOSAURUS

[150–144 million years ago]

VELOCIRAPTOR

[99–65 million years ago]

THERIZINOSAURUS

[85–70 million years ago]

TYRANNOSAURUS REX

[85–65 million years ago]

CORYTHOSAURUS

[80–75 million years ago]

TROODON

[78–76 million years ago]

TRICERATOPS

[72–65 million years ago]

MAJUNGASAURUS

[70–65 million years ago]

Brimming with creative inspiration, how-to projects, and useful information to enrich your everyday life, Quarto Knows is a favorite destination for those pursuing their interests and passions. Visit our site and dig deeper with our books into your area of interest: Quarto Creates, Quarto Cooks, Quarto Homes, Quarto Lives, Quarto Drives, Quarto Explores, Quarto Gifts, or Quarto Kids.

18 19 20 21 22   5 4 3 2 1

ISBN: 978-0-7603-6305-8

Author: LJ Tracosas
Design: Sam Dawson
Illustration: Alex Ries/jupiterartists.com
Editorial: Nicole Burns Ascue, Ruth Austin, and Jill Saginario
Production: Tom Miller
Product development: Peter Schumacher

Printed, manufactured, and assembled in Shenzhen, China, 06/18.

Image Credits—*Sink Your Teeth Into Dinosaurs!*

Front Cover: © Binkski/Shutterstock, © Pinkyone/Shutterstock, © Ratana21/Shutterstock, © Lightspring/Shutterstock; Title Page: © Zepedrocoelho/Shutterstock; Page 2: © ermess/Shutterstock, © Marcio Jose Bastos Silva/Shutterstock, © Maria Arts/Shutterstock, © 2j architecture/Shutterstock; Page 3: © ermess/Shutterstock, © Pinkyone/Shutterstock, © Maria Arts/Shutterstock; Page 4: © ermess/ Shutterstock, © hugolacasse/Shutterstock, © fusebulb/Shutterstock, © Marcio Jose Bastos Silva/Shutterstock, © Pinkyone/Shutterstock, © stockphoto mania/Shutterstock; Page 5: © hugolacasse/Shutterstock, © Pinkyone/Shutterstock, © Ratana21/Shutterstock, © stockphoto mania/Shutterstock, © jörg röse-oberreich/Shutterstock, © Catmando/Shutterstock, © Sofia Santos/Shutterstock; Page 8: © fztommy/ Shutterstock; Page 16: © tristan tan/Shutterstock; Page 24: © Hein Nouwens/Shutterstock, © Aapthamithra/Shutterstock; Page 34: © Aapthamithra/Shutterstock; Page 38: © ZiaMary/Shutterstock; Page 45: © fztommy/Shutterstock; Page 46: © Binkski/Shutterstock, © Pinkyone/Shutterstock, © kstudija/Shutterstock, © Teguh Mujiono/Shutterstock (3); Page 47: © Binkski/Shutterstock, © Pinkyone/ Shutterstock, © kstudija/Shutterstock; Page 48: © Pinkyone/Shutterstock

Design Elements throughout: © Robert Adrian Hillman, © Polina Maltseva/Shutterstock, © pinare/Shutterstock, © Florian Augustin/ Shutterstock, © SCOTTCHAN/Shutterstock, © Natykach Nataliia/ Shutterstock, © Milagli/Shutterstock, © geographlo/Shutterstock, © OK-SANA/Shutterstock

306375